THE GREAT AMERICAN CONSPIRACY

THE ELECTIONS

THAT CHANGED THE DEMOCRACY

The great American conspiracy.

The elections that changed democracy.

Written by César Andrés Muñoz Madrigal in February 2021.

L'Hospitalet de Llobregat, Barcelona, Spain.

TABLE OF CONTENTS

Foreword

In the year 2021 we are still living in turbulent times due to the Covid-19 pandemic, not only due to the health emergency that it entails but also because of the economic consequences that it has and will continue to have in the coming years for most of the nations of the planet.

But we can already speak of the year 2020 in the past, as the year that marked the Covid-19 pandemic, the year that marked the consequent economic crisis in force today, and as the year of the US elections to the presidency of the government on November the 3rd 2020, the result of which has been the entry of the new tenant of the White House, the new president of the Democratic party, Joe Biden.

Obviously, the result of the US presidential elections, being the USA still the most powerful country in the world as of February 2021, that is, in economic, political and military terms, although every time less in comparison to China, should not be underestimated, since the politics and economy of the United States directly influences the policies and economies of practically all the nations of the world due to world globalization, that is, understanding as globalization the phenomenon in which economic, business, social relations are produced, etc. between people and entrepreneurs from different parts of the planet, for example with the possibility of buying products online that come from another country located in another part of the world, or the fact of being able to maintain contact by videoconference through mobile applications with people from other parts of the world, etc. In other words, globalization is about the mostly positive phenomenon of global interconnection at a professional and personal level between people from different countries, in which the decisions of the governments or people of one country have an increasing consequence on the economies and policies of other countries.

But in addition to what happens in the United States affects the rest of the globalized world, what happens in the elections of this nation is also a reflection of what could be happening in the elections of other countries. Thus, the fact that in the United States an alleged electoral fraud may occur, leads us to think about the extent to which it might be occurring in other nations as well, and to what extent there can be real democracy in any nation on the planet, when not even in the United States the elections seem to have been so fair, clean and transparent.

Results of the legal actions of Donald's Trump team and of other US citizens

On February the 9th 2021, some news emerged about the results of the legal actions of the Donald Trump team and other American citizens against the results of the presidential elections of November the 3rd 2020.

So the facts are as follows:

1.One of the most repeated claims is that Donald Trump's legal team began legal actions against the alleged electoral fraud of the November 3rd 2020 elections, which no single court has agreed with. So a recent study shows that such a claim is false.

2. This is reflected in a study prepared by the lawyer John Droz junior, who has been in charge of tracking with his team the legal cases undertaken by the legal team of Donald Trump and other instances of the Republican party.

3. According to the analysis by John Droz Jr. and his team, of the 22 cases that have been heard in court allowing the presentation of evidence, Trump and the Republicans won 15.

4. In other words, 2/3 of the cases that to date have been resolved by the courts through a hearing of both parties, the majority have agreed with Donald Trump and the Republicans.

5. The basis of the study by John Droz Jr. is an investigation into the 81 legal actions that were initiated in connection with the presidential elections of November the 3rd 2020 and that goes until February the 6t[h] 2021.

6. Of the 81 cases, 11 were withdrawn or regrouped and 23 were rejected because of various reasons. According to Droz, these cases cannot be considered as a victory or defeat for either party to the extent that the facts were not analyzed.

7. Of the 27 remaining cases, 22 were concluded after the different arguments had been discussed in court, the evidence had been assessed and a judicial decision was issued.

8. Of those 22 cases in which the allegations were effectively analyzed by the courts and a sentence was passed, Trump and the Republicans won 15 and lost 7.

9. This means, according to Droz, that Trump and the Republicans have won most of the cases related to the 2020 presidential elections which have been judged to the end and thave been the subject of a sentence according to their merits. Droz adds: "Is that what the mainstream media are reporting?".

10. Among the legal victories won by the Republicans and the Trump team is the case "RNC v. Miller" in the courts of Iowa, where the Republican party won a judicial injunction related to the applications of the vote by mail.

11. Another victory was the rare "RNC v. Gill" case also in Iowa, in which the Trump campaign won a judicial injunction, ordering a county official not to distribute or accept signed forms containing pre-printed information.

12. Another legal victory was the "Trump for President vs. Bookyard" legal case in Pennsylvania courts, where a judicial injunction was granted against the counting of votes by mail in places where voters had been allowed to present identification.days after election Day.

13. In a very revealing way, only three procedures were related to the inaccuracies of the vote counting machines. Of those 3, one was rejected because of the jurisdiction, another was rejected although the evidence was not allowed to be examined, and another remains open because the presentation of evidence was authorized.

14. According to Droz, the most plausible explanation for the fact that there were so few cases in these two areas that are legally proving fraud or manipulation in the vote counting machines is that they are processes that consume a lot of time and require substantial research and documentation work. There was simply no time to carry them out before key points in the process were reached, such as the electoral college meeting.

15. Droz points out as the objective of his report that the public needs to be much better educated in relation to the question of the integrity of the elections, and have a better understanding of the component of legal procedures as a key part of it.

16. Until February the 6th 2021, 25 more legal cases remain to be resolved.

Thus, as revealed in the article mentioned above of the Time magazine, the possibility of Donald Trump remaining for a second term in the White House was faced with what

Thus the rumors of an alleged electoral fraud in the presidential elections of the United States on November the 3rd 2020 seemed discredited by an alleged lack of evidence that has been repeated so much in the media, until the same media has written an article about the last presidential elections, revealing the secrets of a conspiracy in the shadows.

Thus, the American magazine "Time" has published an article on the internet dated February the 4th 2021, and on February the 15th it did so in its own magazine, entitled "The Secret History of the Shadow Campaign That Saved the 2020 Election, explaining what were the operations carried out by politicians, unions, the media, social networks, large technology companies, associations for the defense of rights of miscellaneous left, etc. in order to ensure before, during and after the US presidential elections of November the 3rd 2020, the victory of the now president Joe Biden at all costs.

Therefore, it is no longer a conspiracy theory but a fact documented by a magazine of international prestige, which it is obviously pro Biden and the globalist agenda as reflected in his article, but cannot be classified as a conspiracy magazine.

As a globalist agenda, we refer to that agenda that supranational entities such as the World Economic Forum, the Bilderberg Club, the Trilateral Commission, the World Bank, the Council on Foreign Relations, the Group of 30 or G30, etc. promote in order to achieve a single world government imposed with a socialist-communist system, in which sovereign nations are simply mere protectorates under the rule of supranational globalist entities, with the objective, among others, of reducing the world population, since they consider that the world is overpopulated, because population grows faster than resources, according to the theory of the 17th and 18th century Anglican clergyman and British scholar Robert Malthus.

In short, the continuous censorship of Donald Trump on social networks, especially the days before, during and after the US presidential elections of November the 3rd 2020, and "the shadow campaign" in the own words of the magazine "Time "so that Donald Trump would not reelected president, it was done to guarantee the election of a president pro globalist agenda, such as Joe Biden (like Barack Obama, Bill Clinton and all the last democratic party presidents have been, for example) with the collaboration of politicians, the media, social networks, people from the US administration, left-wing groups defending various rights, along with the interference and participation of foreign countries such as China, Iran, Italy, etc. as discussed below.

Even though it has been emphatically stated by the media that the complaints filed by Donald Trump's team of attorneys had no supporting evidence, the truth is that thousands of evidence and hundreds of affidavits (sworn declarations in front of a lawyer) were presented, many of which came from witnesses who witnessed electoral fraud in one way or another, although unfortunately these complaints were not admitted due to an alleged lack of evidence, which It is not surprising that they were not admitted, since the conspiracy that narrates the Time magazine is of colossal dimensions and would affect all levels of the administration, the media, managers of the business world and all kinds of left-wing associations.

However, the reality today is different, since of 22 legal cases related to electoral fraud presented by Donald Trump's legal team and the Republicans in different courts, which have admitted the evidence and in which it has been dictated judgment, they have won 15 of these cases and lost 7 of them, which is a victory in court in 2 out of 3 cases. A victory that by the way is late for Trump to run for re-election as president, obviously is a total victory for these national conspirators in the shadows though.

So the title of this book "The great American conspiracy. The elections that changed democracy "arises from the fact that this conspiracy was perpetrated by internal conspirators of the United States, which also allowed external nations to interfere in the elections, that is, it is an American conspiracy against America.

In a significant way, what has happened in the United States elections is a reflection of the health of democracy in the world, and of what may be happening with the elections in other nations. For this reason, these US elections on November the 3rd 2020 "have changed democracy", or have reflected the true state of democracy that we had believed to be so healthy in Western nations.

1

Introduction

Basically we can find three types of actors who have been the protagonists of this conspiracy, fraud and manipulation of the results of the US elections of November 3rd, 2020:

1. Internal agents: mass media, social networks, union organizations, leftist groups, Big Tech (big technology companies like Facebook, Twitter, etc.), part of the US high administration (known as the Deep State), courts, the CIA (US Central Intelligence Agency), etc., most of which appear in the report of the magazine "Time" published on the internet on February the 4th, 2021 and that appeared in the same magazine on February 15t[h] 2021 : "The secret history of the shadow campaign that saved the 2020 elections".

2. Internal-external actors: vote counting computer companies such as Smartmatic and Dominion, Scytl, etc. who have directors, shareholders and servants outside the United States, and who have also previously worked in the elections of other nations such as Venezuela. These companies have developed vote counting software very similar to each other, which is highly vulnerable to cyberattacks, since in order to work these vote counting machines need to be connected to the internet, which makes them highly vulnerable to cyberattacks by foreign hackers.

3. External actors: computer hackers from China, Iran, Italy, and other countries before, during and after the elections of November the 3rd 2021, who passed votes from Donald Trump to Joe Biden.

It is thanks to the sum of these three types of actors that there was such a big success in the conspiracy for Joe Biden to win the elections.

2

Internal actors of the electoral conspiracy.

The internal conspiracy in the shadow.

As we have already indicated in the prologue, the internal actors of the electoral fraud in the United States presidential elections of November the 3r^d 2020, are mentioned in the Time magazine report published online on February the 4th 2021, with the title "The Secret History of the Shadow Campaign that saved the 2020 election", report that can be found at the following link: https://time.com/5936036/secret-2020-election-campaign/ where the following facts are told:

1. The magazine "Time" tells in a triumphalist tone with this report how the coalition that prevailed over Donald Trump was formed in the elections of November the 3rd 2020.

2. This report has been written by Leslie Dickstein, Mariah Espada, and Simone Shah.

3. Time magazine presents the formation of this coalition and its action as an operation to save democracy.

4. Time magazine points out that after the November the 3rd elections, nothing happened. Contrary to the idea that leftist demonstrations were going to break out and degenerate into violence, they did not take place.

Second, the business world turned against Donald Trump, who did not understand what was happening.

5. Time magazine notes that there was a conspiracy going on behind the scenes, which stopped the protests and coordinated the resistance of the CEOs (Chief Executive Officers). Both surprises were the result of an informal alliance between left-wing activists and business moguls.

6. This pact between the left and big business was formalized in a pact through a joint note of the United States Chamber of Commerce and the AFL-CIO, which is the largest union group in the United States, a note that was published the same day of the elections. Such a pact is literally presented by Time magazine as a union of the forces of labor and capital to keep the peace and oppose Donald Trump's assault on democracy.

7. Time magazine notes that while much of this activity took place on the ideological left, it was separate from the Biden campaign, and crossed ideological lines with crucial contributions from conservative, non-party actors.

According to Time, the goal was not to stop Trump's victory but to avoid an election so dire that no outcome at all could be discerned.

8. According to Time, this work touched on all aspects of the elections. They got states to change voting systems and laws, and helped secure hundreds of millions in public and private funding, sidelined voter suppression demands, recruited armies of poll workers, and got millions to vote by mail for the first time.

They successfully lobbied social media companies to take a tougher line against what they call "disinformation." And after Election Day they watched for any pressure points to make sure that Trump couldn't turn the result around.

9. Time magazine insists that these facts must be known so that it is seen that the conspirators were not rigging the elections but were "strengthening" them.

10. Time magazine points out as the architect of the conspiracy the Jewish trade unionist Mike Podhorzer, an unknown person outside the United States, with little media coverage in America, but who for almost a quarter of a century was a senior adviser to the AFL-CIO , which is the largest union federation in the United States.

At the beginning of the 21st century Podhorzer created "the Analyst" Institute, which according to Time magazine is a secret firm that applies scientific methods to political campaigns. Podhorzer was also instrumental in founding "The Catalist", a data management company situated on the ideological left.

11. In October 2019 Podhorzer seemed to realize that Donald Trump would win re-election, not least because of the support he received from blue-collar workers (workers at the bottom of the corporate hierarchy, such as the performers of manual tasks or laborers) once controlled by the AFL-CIO, and so expressed it in a circular sent that same month.

12. Podhorzer's concern coincided with the action of other entities such as the "Democracy Defense Coalition", racial groups and officials, and concluded with the certainty that the totally decentralized American electoral system in states could be used to achieve their ends. Thus, on March the 3rd 2020, Podhorzer wrote a memorandum in this regard entitled "Threats to the 2020 elections."

13. The arrival of Covid-19 led Podhorzer to reaffirm himself in the idea that Trump could continue as president, and he began to hold meetings with what the Time magazine calls the "progressive universe." Universe that according to Time magazine was made up of the union movement, the institutional left such as Planned Parenthood and Greenpeace, resistance groups such as "Indivisible" and "Move on", data sources of progressive strategies, representatives of donors and foundations, popular organizers statewide, racial justice activists and others.

This coalition according to Time magazine was strengthened by the racial protests that took place in the summer of 2020.

14. Faced with the need for funding in March 2020, the coalition appealed to Congress to provide funds to the electoral administration from funds destined for the fight against Covid-19. Thus, more than 150 organizations requested 2,000 million US dollars from the United States Congress. That month the Cars Act (Organization in charge of legislating the statute or law to prevent children and animals from being injured when they travel by car) gave 400 million dollars to the administrators of state elections, but according to Time magazine it was not enough. Among others who donated was the Chan Zuckerberg Initiative (The Chan Zuckerberg Initiative, with Mark Zuckerberg being the creator of Facebook) which gave another 300 million dollars.

15. Only one of the institutes involved raised money to promote in 37 different states, including the state of Washington DC, the vote by mail that was seen absolutely essential for the defeat of Trump.

The Voter Participation Center in August and September 2020 sent out vote-by-mail applications to 15 million people living in key states.

16. The result of the coalition's activities was spectacular because in the 2020 elections almost half of the vote was by mail, and only a quarter of the voters did so in the usual way, in person and on election day.

17. Along with controlling the voting system, the coalition was in charge of controlling the media, an action that the Time magazine also presents as a defense of democracy. The role played by Laura Quinn, one of the founders of "The Catalist" could have been essential since she had a project that dealt with tracking information on social media platforms. Given that anti-coalition information could be generalized, the way out that Quinn saw was to pressure the platforms to remove content or stories that she believed contained disinformation.

Quinn acknowledges that this policy of pressuring social media platforms had never been applied on these platforms until then.

18. According to Time magazine in November 2019, Mark Zuckerberg, founder of Facebook, met at a dinner held at his home with civil rights leaders who insisted on the need to control the content on social media platforms.

Vanita Gupta, president and CEO of the "Leadership Conference on Civil and Human Rights" had a relevant role in this lobby theory in front of Facebook and Twitter. Gupta was appointed by President Obama as the United States Attorney for Civil Rights, and has received the nomination by Joe Biden for appointment as Associate State Attorney General.

19. According to Time magazine, this coalition was also joined by officials, public officials and military leaders. Members of the Republican party opposed to Trump ideas also participated.

A week before the election, the United States Chamber of Commerce joined the conspiracy, a step that ended with the joint statement on Election Day.

20. Election night, according to Time magazine, got off to a desperate start for Democrats. Thus Donald Trump was ahead in the elections winning easily in the states of Florida, Ohio and Texas, and practically being able to claim the victory in Michigan, Wisconsin and Pennsylvania.

At 11 p.m. at a meeting on Zoom, many members of the coalition spoke out on terror, so Podhorzer reassured them, and just then the Fox network surprised everyone by announcing that Biden had won in the state of Arizona. According to Time magazine the campaign had worked.

21. During the following days, the pressure from the coalition was directed especially against Republican politicians so that they would not invalidate those results, which was about to happen, for example, in Michigan. It was through these pressures, in which the media and social media platforms such as Twitter played an important role, that the results of states such as Pennsylvania or Wisconsin were certified in a favorable way for Joe Biden.

22. Despite all the above, Time magazine points out that the coalition did not fully triumph until January the 6th 2021, when the violent entry into the Capitol took place, whose responsibility "Time" magazine attributed to Donald Trump, which has already been discredited in the second failed impeachment against Donald Trump by the

Democratic party filed in January 2021 and with the voted decision in favor of Trump by the United States Senate on February the 13t^h 2021 , as he did not instigate entry into the Washington D.C. Capitol.

23. Time magazine claims that today left-wing activists pressure Democrats for left-wing policies, business leaders announce that they will not donate money to legislators who refused to certify favorable results for Biden, Podhorzer and their Allies continue to meet, and Trump had to face his second impeachment even after having ceased as a president, which is illegal, since impeachment is a political trial that can only be made against an active president and not against a former president.

24. Time magazine concludes the report by pointing out that democracy won in the end and that the will of the people prevailed.

Statements at a press conference by Donald Trump's legal team and other statements

Rudy Giuliani, a lawyer for Donald Trump's legal team, pointed out at a press conference on November the 20th 2020 that they had Democratic party witnesses about electoral fraud, a thousand sworn statements under sentence of jail, early morning trucks with illegal votes, zombie ballots (of deceased people who allegedly had voted), corrupted election attorneys, evidence of manipulated Dominion Voting Systems software, and votes of non-existent people.

<u>A Democratic prosecutor confesses</u>

In the exposition of the facts, the name of Jesse Jacob showed up. She is a Detroit Democratic official that witnessed and said on sworn declaration "affidavit", that several authorities of her city council taught her how to commit fraud in this 2020 election. The woman reveals that she was trained to change the envelopes of the postal ballots that arrived out of date so that they would appear as delivered before the 3th of November 2020. They used this ruse to vote for tens of thousands of votes and not only would she be involved, "we have many more confessing officials and people from the environment," Giuliani clarified,

<u>Early morning trucks in Michigan</u>

But in Michigan even more crimes were committed, and very serious ones, Giuliani pointed out. In the thread of the affidavits, two electoral attorneys, who were at the voting tables, describe that they saw a truck that was not from the Postal Service, with employees who were not wearing their work uniforms either.

They were struck by the fact that that vehicle appeared out of nowhere and at 4.30 h in the morning. And what happened? Well, as officials comment, suddenly thousands of ballots left the truck. The alleged workers brought some 100,000 votes by mail to Detroit and coincidentally 100% of all the votes were for Joe **Biden**. The evidence also indicates that it would not be the only truck that appeared incognito with unexpected votes.

But it is that not only these three electoral prosecutors admit that there was corruption, but Giuliani confirmed that he had more than 200 affidavits of this type that corroborate these criminal and premeditated acts. Among them were other table prosecutors who saw tens of thousands of votes being processed not just once, but up to five times. In other words, the same ballot counted on the machines up to five times and in view of other officials, as stated, for example, by Melissa Carone, a "freelance" computer worker, who worked in the presidential elections for the company Dominion Voting Systems within the IT support team, which was the provider of many vote counting machines in many states.

<u>Corruption in Pennsylvania</u>

This same operation would have occurred in Michigan, Wisconsin, Nevada, Georgia and Pennsylvania. "The 90% of the votes that came after the date of the elections to the different cities of the states were for Biden. It is absurd", criticized Giuliani, Donald Trump's lawyer.

Furthermore, the colossal evidence-gathering work of this elite of lawyers did not stop. In the two weeks following the November the 3rd election, affidavits were signed by hundreds of Democratic and Republican observers and prosecutors. So the former mayor of New York speaks of "a systematic fraud scheme in cities controlled by Democrats and with a history of corruption."

<u>19th century voters</u>

And it seems that everything was worth it, since the dead never participated so much in an election as in 2020. So there were voters who were born in 1850, 1900, etc.

Also in Pennsylvania, Trump's defense lawyers have found that 15,000 people were disappointed when they went to vote since other individuals had already voted for them on November the 3rd 2020.

Based on the affidavits (sworn statements) presented, the table prosecutors declare that they were taught and received orders from the Democratic authorities to vote for the people who had not gone to the tables. But when they found that those who were not going to vote did it, a great uproar was formed. And that is how the lawyer Giulani declared that he had all the evidence despite the media saying otherwise.

<u>Wisconsin</u>

In Milwaukee, the lawyer describes what happened as in other states. The Republican observers that were sent were not allowed to be in the electoral process. And so the lawyers of **Trump** found up to 100,000 votes from people who are not registered anywhere. Who are they? It seems that they are made up names.

Those illegal votes should have been eliminated, but "by chance", they all went to Joe Biden and were counted. If these illegal votes had not been registered, Trump would have won Wisconsin. Let us remember that here the counting also stopped, the mysteries began, and Biden thus beat Trump by 30,000 good votes, who just began winning in this state after the counting stopped.

Another piece of evidence in the state of Wisconsin is that there was an overvoting in Milwaukee. The researchers found that there were more votes than people registered in the city. "We have districts with 200% and up to 300% overvoting," Giuliani defended.

Finally, in Georgia, another of the key states, Giuliani reported that they were going to file another lawsuit. In this state, according to Giuliani, there had been a count but done in his own way, and there was no audit, so the lawyer knew that they were not going to expose the illegal votes. And here they also had numerous affidavits. In them they alleged "having been thrown out of the tables and not being able to see the ballots clearly." The same thing happened in Arizona.

Smarmatic and Dominion

The role of the software of Smarmatic, a subsidiary of Dominion Voting System, is also fundamental in the fraud and was part of it, said former Donald Trump attorney and former federal prosecutor, Sidney Powell. The scandal would be worldwide. Trump's lawyer claimed to have confidants from the company who had signed affidavits, as reported by another Trump attorney, Lin Wood.

"Numerical deviations in the votes are mathematically impossible. For example, 186,000 votes came in all of a sudden and they were all for Biden. I'm not talking about a curve anymore, but about massive vertical peaks, right after the counting was stopped. There Dominion intervenes injecting the necessary votes into the system. These machines are hackable and we can prove it. The elections were fraudulent in Venezuela and Argentina, in order for their corrupt politicians to perpetuate themselves in power. Well, they are not going to intimidate us, we are going to uncover the biggest case of political corruption ", concluded Powell visibly moved.

Criticism of the shadow conspiracy

In the first place, Time magazine tells what it calls "conspiracy" to prevent Trump from remaining president, but it does not do so in a negative way, but rather presents the process as an immense task carried out in the shadows to save democracy. In other words, he equates the salvation of democracy with the eviction of Trump from the White House, and of this statement that the Time magazine finds so evident, he does not present either clarification or justification.

In addition, although the Time magazine presents voting by mail as the optimal solution for elections, it does not give any reason why this system was the most suitable for voting. Should we perhaps understand that voting by mail was favored to guarantee that the greatest number of people could vote in a situation dominated by fear of contagion by the coronavirus? However, it is known that voting by mail is more easily manipulated or changed, that is, it offers fewer guarantees than voting in person and has been the subject of a lot of accusations of electoral fraud, and these accusations have been very numerous due in part to that practically half of the voters did it by this means.

Secondly, starting from this principle which is debatable at least, the Time magazine considers it appropriate to describe the campaign in the shadows aimed at displacing Donald Trump from power. This conspiracy would have started in the mind of Mike Podhorzer, a character hardly known but of considerable weight in the action of the largest union federation in the United States, as well as in the development of electoral strategies, and later it would have spread to add in as well the big capital (the CEOs of different big companies), to NGOs such as Planned Parenthood or Greenpeace, racial organizations, the media and the big technology companies known as "Big Tech".

The result was undoubtedly spectacular. Thus, first there was a series of actions so that the vote would be mainly by mail, taking advantage of the fact that each state has its own voting system and preventing Republican attempts to ensure that those systems had guarantees. Finally almost half of the votes in the USA presidential elections on November the 3rd 2020 ended up being by mail

Second, funds supposedly destined for the fight against the coronavirus would have been diverted towards the establishment of armies of employees related to the electoral process.

Third, the media and especially social networks would have been able to censor any type of content that went against the theses of the coalition and favorable to Donald Trump. Again, as in the case of the postal vote, it was an unprecedented event.

Fourth, a joint agreement between the big capital and the great union confederation against Donald Trump would have been reached on the same day as the elections.

Fifth, local politicians were allegedly pressured to certify the results that benefited Joe Biden.

Sixth. the entire process on January the 6th 2021 would have been finished by presenting Trump as the direct person responsible for the entry of protesters into the Capitol.

Seventh, the weight of the coalition members who pressure the Democratic Party to adopt measures from the left, which intend to maintain the prevalence of the mail vote and flawed counting systems, would have been maintained to this day, and they intend that social networks continue to maintain their content censorship. In other words, they intend that nothing will ever be the same and that the mechanisms that gave them victory over Donald Trump will be maintained forever

To pretend that these drastic and threatening changes be perpetuated and also present them as an achievement and a victory, and even as the salvation of democracy is at least striking but has its logic. Thus, the fact that Donald Trump's legal team might have presented evidence of electoral fraud in the Senate during the second impeachment, and the fact that certain actions are to be enshrined as normal political actions, may be behind the fact that the Time magazine publishes a report like this and also does it in a boastful tone, as if it were writing about the action of pristine citizens concerned about the preservation of democracy instead of how the coalition of forces willing to impose their interests on the citizens regardless of the will of these.

Unfortunately, instead of finding ourselves with a confession of part or with a story of salvation of democracy, what emerges from this report is a great betrayal of the essential principles of any democratic system. It is a betrayal that passes through conspiracy, through the alliance of the powerful to impose themselves on the popular will, through the manipulation of the media to skew information, through the censorship of social media platforms so that they present a single speech favorable to the conspiracy, and by the pressure on politicians and officials to certify more than dubious electoral results.

However, despite its immense dimensions, this great betrayal will not be recognized as such by those who committed it, because when the betrayal triumphs, no one dares to call it treason.

Finally, it seems that Time magazine has published this report with the intention of anticipating Donald Trump's legal team, which was expected to take advantage of his second "impeachment" to present evidence of electoral fraud.

The history of Dominion and Smartmatic

Dominion Voting Systems was created in 2003, being responsible for the computer registration system in most of the United States, and is a Canadian company whose US headquarters are in Denver, Colorado.

They currently run the electronic voting system in 28 states, including Michigan, Pennsylvania and Wisconsin where there were numerous reports of voter fraud by the Donald Trump team.

Rudy Giulani, who belonged to Donald Trump's legal team, already rightly said in a press conference in November 2020, that the system was prepared to commit fraud, but it was not prepared to receive so many votes from Donald Trump, and that is why the electoral fraud could be proved.

In fact, already in the 2016 presidential elections, Dominion, according to a study by the Wharton Business Agency, which studied its hardware and software records, passed 71 million American votes.

On the other hand, Smartmatic is a company founded in Delaware, United States, by Venezuelan engineers, and whose voting machines and software have already served to manipulate electoral results. So Dominion has precisely manipulated the results of the elections in Venezuela as declared on November the 15t^h 2020 in Dallas, Texas in a sworn statement or "affidavit" by a former member of the government of Hugo Chávez, confirming that the Smartmatic software was created and exported in order to steal elections, as this has happened already in Venezuela's and Argentina's elections.

A summary of what is said by this former member of the government of Hugo Chávez in this affidavit is as follows: "The conspiracy against the United States began more than 10 years ago in Venezuela, and from there it spread throughout the world. The goal is to win and maintain the power of the elite and involve politicians, multinationals and anyone who wants to avoid freedom. I was selected as a security member of the President of Venezuela. I witnessed the creation of a sophisticated electronic voting system that allowed Venezuelan rulers to manipulate the vote. The conspiracy of which I am an eyewitness refers to President Chávez, the head of the National Electoral Council, Jorge Rodríguez Gómez, and the directors of Smartmatic. The objective was to create a software that would allow the votes against Chávez to be exchanged for votes in his favor. Chávez met with all these guys, including myself, to create the electoral manipulation software. Chávez offered many incentives, including large sums of money. The software created was called the Electoral Management System and was intended for the use of voting machines connected to the network (internet), and therefore maneuverable.

Those who voted were recognized by fingerprints and this was to give credibility to the whole system. Chávez was very insistent that the vote could be manipulated without being caught, and he got it from Smartmatic.

After the system was created, I have seen it used in various elections. For example in the 2006 election against Rosales. But in particular, the election that I saw absolutely altered with this system was that of 2013, used by Chávez for Maduro to be elected.

Looking at the screens in real time we could see how they worked because the numbers of votes were constantly changing in seconds in favor of Maduro. At two in the afternoon, Radonsky was ahead of Maduro by two million votes. At this time Smartmatic, through the connection to the internet and by order of Maduro, made that all the counts were cleared in all areas of the country and millions of votes were moved in favor of Maduro. It took them about two hours to do everything looking like an internet blackout, while manipulating the data and looking directly at the voting machines where there were more votes for Maduro's opponent. When they declared that the internet and the count were working again, they had already changed everything with an advantage for Maduro of about 200,000 votes. After Smartmatic created this software, Chávez exported it to all parts of Latin America and when Chávez died, Smartmatic was the only one who could manipulate the elections. Smartmatic is the DNA of all types of electronic voting, including Dominion. Dominion and Smartmatic have done business together in the USA. The software is essentially the same and works identically. In 2017, during Maduro's new elections, Mr. X publicly stated what Smartmatic did in the previous elections, saying that everything was rigged. He recognized in all aspects what happened in the 2020 US presidential elections with what he witnessed in the 2013 elections in Venezuela. " including Dominion. Dominion and Smartmatic have done business together in the US The software is essentially the same and works identically."

In 2017, during Maduro's new elections, this very same Mr. X publicly stated what Smartmatic did in the previous elections, saying that everything was rigged. He recognized in all aspects what happened in the 2020 US presidential elections with what he had witnessed in the 2013 elections in Venezuela. "

Later the Carter Foundation went to evaluate the legality of the electoral process of those Venezuelan elections of 2013, but the evaluation by the Foundation of this former president of the United States was not a guarantee of much, since among other reasons the employees of this foundation are neither statistics experts nor computer scientists.

Finally, we would like to add that in a very significant way many Dominion employees since November the 3r^d 2020 have deleted their profiles from the professional social network LinkedIn. In fact, Dominion is a Canadian company, and it seems to be just a cover company which they might have wanted to be looked at or blamed to, since the great international company behind Dominion is Smartmatic. And perhaps there might have been members within Trump's attorneys who participated in the misinformation. In fact, a group of Trump lawyers left Trump's legal team, and Giulani stated that there were people who could not withstand the pressure.

<u>Is there a shareholder relationship between Dominion and Smartmatic</u>?

At first it seems that there is no shareholder relationship but the problem is much greater than the fact that they may have crossed shares between them. The key to the relationship between them is a North American company called "Sequoia Voting Systems" that was bought by Smartmatic in 2005, a year after manipulating the reversal referendum that allowed Chávez to stay in power.

So the first three contracts with the Bolivarian government amounted to 120 million US dollars and that was when it bought Sequoia. And what did Smartmatic do with Sequoia? Smartmatic improved the software and used it for electoral processes in other countries, for example in Argentina, also reporting electoral fraud.

Moreover, in the United States in 2016, Sequoia voting machines were used in the March primary elections of Chicago and the newspaper "The Washington Post" reported that there was a high risk of fraud in those elections, speaking about this company and about the link between Smartmatic and Hugo Chávez or the Chavista executive system, a link that Washington Post journalists now deny.

Even the government of the United States itself investigated Smartmatic through the Foreign Investment Committee. So Caroline Maloney, who was a Democratic representative for the New York State, said that the government should know who owns their voting machines, and that it was a national security problem because with the Sequoia software enhanced by Smartmatic they could steal their elections. In this way, in the face of criticism, the directors of Smartmatic sold Sequoia to Dominion Voting Systems, which was a small and almost recently created Canadian company, which is the one that has been under suspicion after the complaints of Donald Trump's lawyers for electoral fraud.

That is why when Donald Trump's legal team spoke of a source from the Hugo Chávez government warning them to be careful with Smartmatic, it is because this person knew that Smartmatic is an expert in manipulating elections. So Smartmatic is a global company with headquarters in London, offices in 12 countries which works in countries such as Argentina, the United States, Belgium, Singapore, the United Kingdom, etc. participating in many electoral processes.

So Smartmatic and Dominion in order to defend themselves against the accusations by Donald Trump's legal team, that is, Rudy Guliani and Sidney Powell, said that they do not share any resources between them. But according to the press releases that Dominion published on June the 4th 2010 when it bought Sequoia from Smartmatic, Dominion bought all the software and all the hardware, along with all the intellectual property from Smartmatic.

Thus, according to the position of many countries and in many cases presenting notorious evidence, it is an ideal software and hardware to commit all kinds of electoral manipulations. In fact, there is nothing that can guarantee that through the hardware and software of Smartmatic and Dominion electoral fraud may not be committed, since in addition their vote counting machines work connected to the internet, which allows them to be easily hacked by cyberattacks. In fact, Venezuelans know well that a real audit of the Smartmatic machines was not allowed, which is what Donald Trump criticized. In fact, hacking into these electoral systems is very simple, and it could even be done by a child who may know a little bit of IT programming.

So then we should ask ourselves who is the president of Smartmatic in order to delve deeper into this story of alleged electoral fraud.

So visiting Smartmatic's own website in the "Us" (Our Team) section indicates that the chairman of the US board of directors is Peter Neffenger, who is a decorated reserve vice admiral of the US coast guard who worked in Barack Obama's cabinet as head of the Transportation Security Administration. In fact, he has always worked for the US security department, and was also on Joe Biden's transition team as a volunteer. Thus, his work in this transition team consisted of supporting one of the review teams of the incoming Administration agency in December 2020 and January 2021, specifically assigned to the Department of Homeland Security.

So as you can see Peter Neffenger as other key people of Smartmatic are people who have held relevant public positions but unknown to the vast majority of people in the world, that is, people who are part of the Deep State, this is part of the administration controlling in the shadows what happens in the politics and administration of the nation, understanding as "deep state" as a form of clandestine government in a nation, operated through networks of covert power groups..

Even the New York Times newspaper has said that the electoral fraud theories are false, but obviously they know that they are not, because these mainstream media are the first to know that these pieces of news are neither false nor theories, and this is why this is so serious. So it seems quite clear to think that the big media, editorial media and social media have orders from higher positions to publish that there has been no electoral fraud.

But in fact Associated Press is the news agency responsible for almost 80% of the publication of international information in the world, which is precisely the agency that has proclaimed the victory of Joe Biden from the beginning.

Thus, on the same official website of Dominion Voting Systems there are many links that lead to the United States Department of Homeland Security, which can also lead to suspicion that they have exclusive close relationships with the United States Administration, that is, Dominion could have an exclusive relationship with the American deep state or directly be part of the American "deep state".

Thus both Smartmatic and Dominion refer to the verifications carried out by international means of their process, such as those carried out by the New York Times or the Associated Press themselves. And what legitimacy does the New York Times or the Associated Press news agency have to know if they have manipulated the electronic vote or the physical vote registry in the United States? In fact, for the verification of the votes, computer and statistical experts are necessary. Thus, the elections in Venezuela have been analyzed for years, specifically since the 2004 elections in Venezuela by statistical experts who have realized that following the laws of large numbers there is something that does not add up, that is to say that the elections in Venezuela have been manipulated by a machine.

It seems clear that the courts have not accepted the complaints not because of lack of evidence and of evidence but because they have orders not to accept them, and to say that there is no reason for these complaints. So the Supreme Court of the United States rejected a lawsuit filed by Texas and backed by the formeroPresident Donald Trump that sought to override the results of the vote in four key states. In its writing, the court has stated that "Texas has not shown a judicially recognizable interest in the manner in which other states conducted the elections. The rest of the motions are rejected as irrelevant."

The nine members of the Supreme Court, including three appointed by the Republican president, concluded that Texas had no right to interfere in the organization of elections in other states.

The Texas' lawsuit against four key states in the election of November the 3rd was intended to override the voting from the territories where Biden won by a narrow margin and were instrumental in guaranteeing his victory: Michigan, Georgia, Pennsylvania and Wisconsin.

The magistrates rejected the request through a brief order, which had been filed as allowed in some cases of litigation between states under a legal doctrine called "original jurisdiction." But the order stated that Texas has no legal capacity to file the claim.

It also turns out that this electronic voting giant called Smartmatic belongs to another company called SGO. This company was founded in 2014 by the manager of Smartmatic, Antonio Múgica, and by Lord Malloch Brown, who is the real key to the matter and about whom nobody talks about .

In fact Lord Mallock, George Soros, Smartmatic and those who make the decisions also have very important ties to the Republican Party, since at the present time there is really no political right or left. In fact, Donald Trump has always been alone going against the globalist system and institutions.

And what need did Donald Trump have to be claiming during the months after the elections that there had been electoral fraud? In fact, he was fighting to the end to try to get the electoral fraud recognized.

So the enemies of freedom get together regardless of the political party that they support but they always sit at the same globalist tables of the UN, the World Bank, the European Commission, Goldman Sachs, Black Rock, which is the world's largest investment asset management company, Vanguard (along with Blackrock and State Street Corporatives are considered the world's three largest investment fund management companies) undermining democracies through characters like Lord Mallock.

 Of course, 100% electronic and computerized elections are not safer, since in addition to the fact that vote counting machines must be connected to the internet to work properly, which makes them highly vulnerable to cyberattacks, on the other hand also the vote management systems (the software) work with algorithms, which are designed to give a series of results and also according to Trump's team, the engineers who have programmed the algorithm were not prepared for having so many votes in favor of Donald Trump, since the software works with a series of variables and parameters that must be entered, and one of these variables entered was that there should be an approximate voting range of 2.7 million votes, according to Donald Trump.

6

Lord Mark Malloch-Brown

Lord Mark Malloch-Brown is the Global President of Smartmatic. Previously he worked in the UK foreign office, he has done many jobs for the UK government and specifically for Gordon Brown, holding the position of Minister of State in Gordon Brown's Foreign Office, as head of Africa, Asia and the United Nations (UN), which is when he was granted the title of "Lord". He also worked at the World Bank as Vice President of Foreign Affairs, and has worked at the United Nations, first as an administrator of the United Nations Development program, also being chief of staff, whilst later he was named number two of the United Nations, that is to say vice president general of the UN, just below the secretary general at that time who was Kofi Annan.

He is also one of the prominent figures of the World Economic Forum that sponsor the Great Reset, being the head of the Business and Sustainable Energy Commission. So it is surprising that today the vast majority of people do not know who this man is, and simply know characters like George Soros, as defenders and promoters of the globalist agenda. However, Lord Mallock-Brown plays a central role and is a key piece that when you place it in the puzzle, It is noticeable that all the surrounding pieces that seem disconnected, effectively have a connection and a coordination between them in the globalist agenda, since of course Lord Mallock-Brown is a close friend of George Soros, and has been vice president of the Quantum fund group, that it is one of Soros' companies for the management of hedge funds, and that together with the Open Society, also a network of George Soros' NGOs, of which Lord Mallock has also been number two and since the beginning of December 2020 has become its president, are used to spread the globalist agenda.

Furthermore, Mallock-Brown and Soros are such friends that when the former was living in New York during his time at the UN, he lived in one of George Soros' houses.

In fact at the front of his position of responsibility at the UN, Lord Mallock-Brown publicly defended the need for the Open Society to have "carte blanche" (it means in French "white letter", which means to be able to do to whatever they please according to their interests) to leverage the supposedly humanitarian UN missions to do good, to carry out coups and revolutions of all kinds for their own benefit. In fact Soros and Mallock-Brown have also given lectures together that can be found on the internet.

In addition, Mallock-Brown is co-chairman of the International Crisis Group, which is a non-profit institution where Zbigniew Brzezinski sat, who was a National Security advisor within the government of the former United States President Jimmy Carter, who (Carter) used to be part of the Trilateral Commission, which is a private international organization founded in 1973 by David Rockefeller, which brings together prominent personalities in the typical economic and business elites, which is also a globalist supranational entity such as the Bilderberg Club and like any of the other entities founded by David Rockefeller. It is called Trilateral because it includes members from America, Europe and Asia-Pacific, with the inclusion also of members from Japan. So all of this was happening at a time when it was said that it was not that Jimmy Carter had people in his government from the Trilateral Commission, but that the Trilateral Commission had Carter.

Curiously, as a young man Mallock-Brown graduated in journalism and did an internship in the British magazine "The Economist", which as well defends ideas of the globalist agenda.

In addition to this, Lord Mark Malloch Brown is the author of a book entitled " The unfinished global revolution. The limits of nations and the pursuit of a new politics. ", in which he also defends a globalist system, where a supranational oligarchy not democratically elected would rule the world by controlling the nations that would disappear or that would become mere protectorates.

In fact, in an interview on a Philippine television channel, which can still be found on YouTube, just before the elections were held there and in which Malloch Brown was the external representative of Smartmatic, which was the company that was going to install its hardware and software systems for the voting management of the Philippine elections, said that the hardware and software licenses of Smartmatic and Dominion are the same, which is what both Smartmatic and Dominion deny after the US presidential elections on November the 3rd, 2020. In addition, as he has said publicly and has written in the German magazine Der Spiegel, he has promoted the idea of legalizing the opium trade in Afghanistan. Later he did it in the UK government together with Gordon Brown, and wanted to create a kind of common agricultural policy, an opium pack, so that the pharmaceutical industries could have morphine almost for free. In fact, George Soros himself is one of the great drivers of the spread of drug use. Thus, the British writer and philosopher Aldous Huxley, who was very intelligent and had very good contacts to know what he was talking about, talked already about how the dictatorships of the future were going to be, saying that they would not need to be violent, and that among other things they were going to be based on the stunning of a large part of the population through drug use.

In fact, it is no longer only a matter of illegal drugs but also legal drugs, since mostly in Western countries there are many people hooked on tranquilizers, antidepressants such as Prozac, etc. The problem, as Huxley himself said, was when they stopped taking that drug, not because of the withdrawal syndrome but because people realized of real life, and then the suffering was unbearable for them.

In this sense, George Soros took advantage of the crisis in Afghanistan, and according to the writer and former Russian intelligence agent Daniel Estulin, both Mallock-Brown and Soros were involved in the Georgian Rose Revolution, which was not a revolution that emerged from the people but imposed by a globalist oligarchy. This revolution began with mass protests over the country's controversial parliamentary elections and ended with the resignation of the then president, Eduard Shevardnadze, which marked the end of the soviet leadership in the country

So Soros has overthrown governments in Eastern Europe and summarizing what happened, when the United Nations with Mallow-Brown as a representative allowed it, then Soros came and took over the governments of Eastern Europe, and a consulting firm called Soller Miller would determine how the heritage and resources of those nations would be privatized in order to loot them. And who was the main international partner of this consulting firm? Indeed, the main international partner was Lord Mallock-Brown. That is to say, they always put the same agents in the front line to plunder nations.

So we see once again that while George Soros is known by many people, Lord Mallock-Brown, despite being a key figure in international strategic geopolitics, is practically unknown to anyone, and basically the explanation is that the mass media report about other news and other personalities of the international politics scene, but not precisely what they should report on, but what interests certain sources of power, that are basically those who pay them or grant them subsidies and public aid.

In addition, on the official Smartmatic website there is an article by Mallock-Brown in which he talks about the need to modernize the United Kingdom's electoral system, because in theory it is failing our democracy, "extremely dangerous for our democracy", which is a very fashionable phrase used by the media and on the internet since many journalists in a significant way speak using this phrase or some other ones with the same meaning. So Lord Mallock-Brown says that the current electoral system does not work, and that there is no real democracy, also adding that when there are online banking transactions or they even book their flights through an App, then we must consider that the elections also They are done without being in person and using physical ballots to cast the votes.

However, face-to-face elections using paper ballots are the only way that may often prevent electoral fraud, even if it seems counterintuitive. It is not possible to always prevent voter fraud, but at least face-to-face elections offer some guarantees that It will not happen.

7

External actors of the electoral conspiracy

<u>The Barcelona company Scyt</u>

Scytl, a provider of electronic voting systems and electoral technology, managed the vote recounting in the November 3rd elections, subcontracted together with other companies by entities of the Federal Government of the United States. His management ranged from voter registration to the counting of votes, carried out at its headquarters in Barcelona and at its headquarters in Frankfurt.

Despite being widely unknown, Scytl managed vote recounting in the 2019 Spanish, Costa Rican or European general elections, in addition to the 2020 US presidential elections. Scytl has also been an electronic ballot delivery service provider for the US Federal Government and at a state level also for Alaska, Arkansas, Kentucky, Mississippi, West Virginia and New York.

Its presence in the United States dates back to 2008 through multiple projects to "modernize the elections", which did not prevent Scytl from filing a bankruptcy on May the 11th 2020 in the courts of Barcelona, after being unable to achieve an agreement with the banks, public institutions and their suppliers to deal with debts of at least 75 million euros. Neither the agreements carried out in France, Australia, the United Kingdom or Switzerland prevented Scytl from filing bankruptcy, not even the important subsidies granted over the years by institutions such as the European Union or the Spanish Ministry of Industry, Energy and Tourism. Curiously Its insolvency was not an obstacle to being subcontracted as partial manager of the most important elections on the planet, though Scytl denies all this information but its website talks about it.

Faced with the avalanche of information since November the 3rd 2020, Scytl has rushed to deny both being suppliers of counting machines for the North American elections and having headquarters in Frankfurt (and political affiliation). However, Sctyl boasted of its Frankfurt office in a document about its management of the elections to the European Parliament in 2019, still available on its own webpage at the following link: <u>https://www.scytl.com/en/resource/european-parliament-elections-2019-success-case/</u>

<u>Barcelona and Frankfurt, epicenters of suspicion</u>

On November the 10th 2020, at one of the most important press conferences in the political history of the United States, the legal team dedicated to demonstrating widespread election fraud, led by Rudy Giuliani and Sidney Powell, insisted again on **foreign interference in the elections, the confirmation of which would entail very harsh penalties for their authors**. Specifically, the former mayor of New York has once again referred to the Barcelona headquarters of Scytl, outraged that the count was carried out outside the borders of the USA, which has more than evident capacity to manage it.

This is not the first time that lawyers investigating electoral irregularities have pointed to Barcelona as the epicenter of the suspicious recount and to the undeniable headquarters of the company. More controversial, and surely even more key to the matter is everything to do with the office that the company denies being in Frankfurt. According to Louie Gohmert, a member of the House of Representatives, a few days after the elections, special forces of the United States Army entered the headquarters of Scytl in the German city, in which their servers were seized with information capable of changing not only the election results but also generating a much greater impact..

Do these investigations affect Spain?

Although there are several companies accused of interfering in the elections of November the 3rd 2020, beyond Dominion and Smartmatic, Scytl's role seems decisive in the United States but blurred in Spain. In Spain in addition to receiving ministerial grants, the company has managed the data report of the electoral count that corresponds to the Ministry of Interior.

On the other hand, if Giuliani marked Barcelona as a key place of foreign interference in the North American electoral process on a recurring basis, Powell already openly affirmed that these systems had served to switch elections in other countries such as Argentina. Giulani also pointed to those who finance these companies, with explicit references to the Clintons' foundation and George Soros, who (Soros) was the first guest of the Spanish president, Pedro Sánchez, to the Moncloa Palace a few days after the 2018 motion of confidence.

<u>Scylt, Swiss software linked to Dominion voting machines</u>

Scylt, which as we have said is a Spanish provider of electronic voting systems and electoral technology founded in 2001 in Barcelona, Spain, is according to the Swiss-American blogger Neal Sutz, a software bought by the Swiss national postal service, which was implemented directly in the Dominion voting machines which are at the center of the US electoral scandal, directly linked to the magnate George Soros. According to Sutz, Switzerland never informed the Trump Administration of serious flaws in the Scylt software, well known to the Swiss government, adding that it had evidence of the plot that was to be acquired by the lawyers of the former president of the USA, Donald Trump.

<u>The Italian government and the aerospace- IT defense company Leonardo SpA</u>

According to journalist Ricardo Corsetto, director of the Italian newspaper "´L'Unico":
"The Italian government and Prime Minister Guiseppe Conte are directly involved in the
electoral fraud that affected the US elections that led to the pending illegal victory of
Joe Biden" . According to US investigation sources, confirmed by a sworn statement,
affidavit, of Arturo D'Elia, former IT director of the company Leonardo SpA, whose copy
I attach and translate below, confessing on January the 6t^h 2021 that he manipulated
data and implanted virus on the main computers of the Italian company under the
orders of personnel from the United States embassy in Rome to pass votes from
Donald Trump to Biden. Also from this United States Embassy in Rome, they worked
since November the 1st 2020 to coordinate this manipulation and transfer of data from
the votes cast for President Trump to Joe Biden, with the technical complicity of
Leonardo SpA, which is a company owned 31% by the Italian government which
generates more than half of its $ 1 billion in annual revenue from its US-based
subsidiary Leonardo DRS, whose chief executive officer, William Lynn III, was
previously undersecretary of defense during the Clinton administration. Leonardo DRS
is actively pursuing a public listing on the NYSE (New York Stock Exchange) in 2021.

Leonardo SpA, formerly known as Finmeccanica, underwent a name change in
January 2017. According to the people who carried out the data change, whose
operation was carried out under the direction of US intelligence officials at the
American Embassy, they used one of the advanced military specifications of Leonardo
(cyber warfare) satellites to transmit manipulated votes to the servers in Frankfurt and
to the United States, according to the journalist Cesare Sacchetti. Leonardo SpA is the
largest industrial company in Italy and is active in the defense, aerospace and
cybersecurity fields. The largest shareholder is the Italian Ministry of Economy and
Finance, which owns approximately 31% of the shares.

Leonardo-Finmeccanica merged the activities of previously controlled companies such
as AgustaWestland, Alenia Aermacchi, Selex ES, OTO Melara and Wass. Leonardo is
the 10th largest defense company in the world and the third largest in Europe with
defense sector revenue accounting for 68% of its annual revenue. The company is
listed on the FTSE MIB index of the Milan Stock Exchange. The company is structured
in five operating divisions: Helicopters, Aircraft, aerostructures, electronics and cyber
systems for security and information. In the fiscal year 2020, the US government

awarded almost $ 1 billion in cybersecurity, intelligence and defense contracts to Leonardo SpA.

The former president of Leonardo is Gianni De Gennora, who left Leonardo in May 2020.

The CEO of Leonardo SpA, Alessandro Profuma, a former banker who in October 2020 was convicted of the Banca di Monte Paschi di Siena scandal. Alessandro Profumo was appointed by the Gentiioni government and reconfirmed by Prime Minister Giuseppe Conte. Profuma himself was recently sentenced to six years for banking irregularities by Italian courts.

One of the members of the board of directors of Leondardo SpA (2017) was the Professor Guido Alpa, former legal partner of Giuseppe Conte in Rome.

Prime Minister Giuseppe Conte in recent days had been the subject of press articles about plans to establish private intelligence agencies and Conte's administration is believed to have played a key role in the international coup that would have compromised the reelection of President Donald Trump. Additionally Switzerland has recently been accused of complicity in the alleged cyber coup, as claimed by Neal Sutz, who denounced Switzerland's active role in the US presidential fraud.

According to local sources with direct knowledge of these events reporting to Nations in Action, the US non-profit organization for electoral integrity and transparency of public governance, the manipulated data was transmitted from Frankfurt to Rome through the United States Embassy in Via Veneto, granting Rome the central role in the alleged international election plot to revoke the votes cast by American citizens for the next president of the United States, thus creating a constitutional crisis. On the night of November the 3rd (in the United States), at approximately 8 a.m. Italian time, the counting of votes was suspended simultaneously in several key states on the battlefield, as shown by some official videos taken from the closed circuit of the Atlanta electoral college and which has been extensively documented in the daily L'Unico.

At the time, while the fraud had already been widely started, the Leonardo SpA IT hackers realized that "Trump was ahead of Biden by a very large and unexpected amount of votes", so much so that the manipulation was in vain and it was not enough to make him lose.

Sicilian Igzanio Moncada, CEO of FATA SpA, a wholly owned subsidiary of Leonardo SpA, is believed to be a bridge between some secret services and the Italian Business

Association of Beijing, the Italian Business Association of Iran and the Italian Business Association of Qatar. It has been said that Moncada may be a key figure in the planning for eight months of electoral piracy in Italy. It appears that high-ranking personnel from the US Embassy in Italy gave the order to act, coordinating the piracy and developing "new algorithms," claimed the former IT director of Leonardo SpA, Arturo D'Elia, who is a key witness to the electoral fraud, to secure a victory for the then Democratic candidate Joe Biden.

<u>The role of the U.S. Embassy in Rome</u>

The United States ambassador to Italy is Lewis Eisenberg, who is precisely a former member of the world's largest aerospace and defense cyberwar conglomerate based in Italy. Thus Lewis Eisenberg was very critical of President Trump's military withdrawal from the world and very close to the neo-Zionist salons connected to the Goldmann circuit (The Golmann circuit is named after Nahum Goldmann, a Polish-born Israeli Zionist founder and long-time president of the World Jewish Congress. He was also president of the World Zionist Organization).

Three top officials from the US intelligence community landed at Fiumicino's Leonardo da Vinci airport several days before the November the 3rd 2020 US elections. According to a former CIA agent, the three intelligence agents were housed at the United States Embassy in Via Veneto to coordinate piracy operations during the suspension of the electoral count from November 3rd to November the 4t^{h}.

<u>Sworn statement, affidavit, by Arturo D'Elia, former IT director of Leonardo SpA, confessing that he participated in the manipulation of data and transfer of votes from Donald Trump to Joe Biden, signed on January the 6t^h 2021.</u>

Region of Lazio
Country of Italy

I, Prof Alfio D'Urso, Advocate/Lawyer, of Via Vittorio Emanuele, Catania, 95131 Italy, do hereby provide the following affidavit of facts as conveyed in several meetings with a high level army security services official:

Arturo D'Elia, former head of the IT Department of Leonardo SpA, has been charged by the public prosecutor of Naples for technology/data manipulation and implantation of viruses in the main computers of Leonardo SpA in December 2020. D'Elia has been deposed by the presiding judge in Naples and in sworn testimony states on 4 November 2020, under instruction and direction of US persons working from the US Embassy in Rome, undertook the operation to switch data from the US elections of 3 November 2020 from significant margin of victory for Donald Trump to Joe Biden in a number of states where Joe Biden was losing the vote totals. Defendant stated he was working in the Pescara facility of Leonardo SpA and utilized military grade cyber warfare encryption capabilities to transmit switched votes via military satellite of Fucino Tower to Frankfurt Germany. The defendant swears that the data in some cases may have been switched to represent more than total voters registered. The defendant has stated he is willing to testify to all individuals and entities involved in the switching of votes from Donald Trump to Joe Biden when he shall be in total protection for himself and his family. Defendant states he has secured in an undisclosed location the backup of the original data and data switched upon instruction to provide evidence at court in this matter.

I hereby declare and swear the above stated facts have been stated in my presence.

DATED this 6th day of January 2021 at Rome, Italy.

____

General Affidavit

8

External actors in the electoral conspiracy according to cybersecurity experts, computer scientists and lawyers

So Mike Lindell, who is the CEO of the American company "My Pillow", launched on February the 5th 2021 on the independent private channel OANN, the documentary on possible electoral fraud in the presidential elections of November the 3rd 2020, featuring testimonials from various cybersecurity experts, along with forensic evidence of voter fraud and cyberattacks perpetrated by foreign nations.

<u>The testimony of Colonel Phil Waldron</u>

The first testimony was that of Colonel Phil Waldron, who made the following statements in his interview as a cybersecurity expert with Mike Lindell:

"My experience in the military is with influence operations, information operations, information warfare, so to speak.

Yes, we started looking to work with our partners in Dallas, that allied security operations group, by doing an analysis of the data they had, not only in Dominion, but also in SOS-Hart and in several of the other management systems of electronic voting. And we saw many similarities and vulnerabilities in the systems that could be easily manipulated and intercepted. Just as a cyber warfare officer I look for vulnerabilities and ways to attack systems to create a strategic advantage for friendly US forces. And so when we started to look at the vulnerabilities and at all the different ways these electronic voting systems could be intercepted, it became clear that we had a problem for the November 3rd elections. And that led us to spend a lot of time working with Russell Ramsland, getting a lot of historical data and insight. In this way we start working on our own, really doing a lot of money connection exercises, doing basic research. And then I brought our local DHS (Department of Homeland Security) team here in Texas, both the Intelligence and Assessments Division, which collects information for the Department of Homeland Security and for CISA (Cybersecurity and Infrastructure Security Agency), our local system. And we spent quite a bit of time giving them an introduction to what we saw and the vulnerabilities in the ways these systems could be intercepted to change election results at the voting machine level, at the server level and fraud at the local level, which is required to induce the illegitimate vote. Then it comes down to the machine level, which is something you were talking about, concerning the algorithms that are entered directly into the tabs. And we have evidence of that in the state of Georgia, where X number of ballots were passed on and they basically stole 13 percent of the vote from President Trump and put that 13 percent of the vote on Joe Biden, which made a twenty-six percent change in voting. So when you look at the machine level, Dominion's voting tabulator machines, there are so many vulnerabilities in the systems, there are so many fundamental cybersecurity practices that are not enabled, that it basically allows anyone with any technical skill to influence our choices. That strategic level is foreign intelligence, I mean foreign intelligence services. And we have plenty of documented ownership of the Chinese Communist Party, whose equity firm directors control Dominion. We also have in the Chinese Communist Party, the president of the Communist Bank of China, who belongs to a board of directors, and is a member of a private equity firm that owns Dominion.

While I am in the company doing tests, the only company that has access to the code and tests of Dominion's machines and code is in Shenzhen, China. It is a company of the Chinese Communist Party, while the United States government, state governments, county governments, do not have access to the continental code. But I think it is unique fact that a Chinese company run by the Chinese Communist Party has access to the code.

And that's why we started to see that third-tier strategic level of electoral manipulation. Many vote movements have come through direct access to Pennsylvania constituencies, to county tabulation centers in Wisconsin, Michigan, Nevada, Arizona, Georgia, and all of that comes directly from foreign countries. China is the predominant and through Pakistani intermediary proxy servers of the Islamic terror group ISIS.

In fact it is very frustrating that everyone says that all the court cases were lost. Well that's a lie. We have statistics on how many court cases are open, how many were dismissed, you know, that are still standing or in process. But there are only two cases to my knowledge, one in Michigan and one in Georgia, where evidence has been heard and those cases are progressing. The Senate in Arizona heard and saw preliminary evidence, issued a court summons and they are pushing forward with a full forensic audit in Arizona, and that could be available as soon as next week. So it is complex and difficult for people to understand. And if it's hard to understand, people just dismiss it as a conspiracy theory.

We find foreign servers in Barcelona, UK and Frankfurt. We'd seen several, you know, the Toronto server, obviously, which is the Dominion server.

Yes, we were mapping the servers before the elections, we identified the Scytl server in Frankfurt until we even got the address it has in Frankfurt. I think it is the largest or one of the largest in the world. Server nodes, you know, cyber, a communications node is called a "deep dig", in order to see Germany's next cyber moves, and there were several people watching the traffic and its volume that night, and they noticed a significant increase in traffic that night, only due to the volume of information that passes through. And one of the reasons they said traffic was going up was because of the US elections.

I believe, from what I have seen and from the witnesses I have spoken to, that this is a coup, which definitely involved elements within our own country and our own federal government. Definitely part of the coup was aided and instigated by a foreign threat, an enemy nation state.

Yes, I think this attack could not have occurred without internal traitors in the United States, again, we have sworn statements from the CIA and State Department personnel of the Italian embassy participating in this coup (as already written in a previous chapter about). We have the name, email and phone number of a senior Justice Department official who was provided to us by a US attorney. This attorney said that this person was closing any Justice Department or FBI investigation into any election or any election-related investigation, and that he was trying to close court cases and making it to the courts. So, from within our own Justice Department, people were closing active investigations.

On the other hand, the FBI went to question the truckers who delivered the ballot papers and made sworn statements. They harassed Americans, patriotic Americans who denounced these vote-filled trucks in order to prosecute It.

They also denounced the Dominion machines. If you look at military planning factors, these are critical capabilities. A capability is what you need to have to execute your mission or the enemy has to have to execute their mission successfully. So a critical capability for this to happen is the inherent vulnerabilities that were built into Dominion Voting Systems software, which, again, we prove through our work that all of this is directly related to the source, Smartmatic, as the core Dominion's software is from Smartmatic. And they definitely have financial gains for financial reasons based on some of the other investments they have made, especially knowing that Smartmatic's board of directors makes billions of dollars because it owns an air purification company. So if you choose a government and administration that is favorable to your business, and they approve a new green deal, your business is going to make billions of dollars from government mandated air purification systems, from public buildings, from buildings of apartments and industrial complexes. Then you would spend a lot of money up front to make sure the election results are in your best interests. The same thing happens for example with China, since this country could prevent the United States from coming to the defense of Taiwan, which we have already seen signs of.

And all the money that China has made for the Biden family, all the money that they have made and invested in American universities and companies, buying our medical and technical intellectual property, stealing much more than they bought. They are waging a war and people just don't realize that we are under attack.

<h1 style="text-align:center"><u>Russell Ramsland's testimony</u></h1>

Russell Ramsland is a founding member of the Allied Security Operational Group which is based in Dallas, Texas and conducts cybersecurity and cyber forensics and was also interviewed by Mike Lindell for the documentary "Absolute Proof" saying as follows:

"About two years ago, we got some records of the Dallas general election from the central tab server. And people wonder, what are these computer records? For me it was about 1,100 pages. And we were able to look at Adam and we were horrified at what we found, because what we found was that people were getting into the system and they were changing votes. They were deleting databases, they were uploading them again, and it came from remote locations.

This happened in 2018 and the election software SAS, but it is very similar to the Dominion software, since most of these voting companies have software with similar DNA.

In fact, I was horrified because clearly someone was messing with the 2018 primary elections. So we tried to alert the authorities, we brought in a Justice Department prosecutor who ran the cyber group in North Texas, and she was horrified by what we showed her and asked us to make a report and finally send it to the FBI. So we did that and the FBI did nothing about it. So we kept investigating and the more we found, the more horrifying it got. Now all of this kept coming out of Dallas, we tried to get senators to see this and we tried to get state officials to see it too. But we kept working on it on our own without stopping at any time. And we finally got seven members of the "Freedom Caucus" (which could be translated as "Board for freedom", which is a board of certain members of the Republican party) in July 2020 to do a two-hour briefing without staff. And what they saw was absolute proof that this electronic voting system that we have is completely compromised. It can be completely manipulated, and they were also horrified.

Thus Texas rejected Dominion's voting machines and voting software, but Texas uses other voting machines. In fact we use voting machines and software from the company Hart InterCivic headquartered in Austin, Texas and we use the Texas census.

In fact in Texas they rejected Dominion's machines and software and accepted Hart's which is similar, for political reasons and because of the influence of the company that finally takes the service of providing the voting machines and software. So we finally got some investigators, in particular Ron Johnson's Department of Homeland Security Oversight Group, and they were also horrified by what we showed them. And they tried to get CISA, which is the Cyber Intelligence Security Administration within the US Department of Homeland Security. They tried to get CISA to take a look at the system, but they didn't want to make the effort of looking at it or taking the risk of doing it. They couldn't be less interested, so we weren't quite sure what to do.

We were also starting to find some media outlets who wanted to start talking about this and they were horrified. But the breakup really came in early August, when we got together some members of the Department of Homeland Security in Austin to look at it and a division, the Intelligence and Analysis Division, to take a look at what we had. And that's the division that handled integrity in the elections before it was handed over. So they looked at it and were horrified and sent a whole team to our store. We spent 11 hours with them, they asked us if we would pass on our data, and of course we did, which they took to Austin. Without us knowing it, the data from our investigations were passed on to three private cyber groups who analyzed it and said: "Are these guys crazy? I mean, is this crazy or is something weird going on here?".

In fact all three groups looked at our data and all three groups came back saying that we were not only right in our observations but that it was terrible.

It is terrible because there is no effective security for the votes. The votes are stored abroad, where they can be easily stored. Twenty-seven states use what is called a "Clarity Sign" to report on Election Night. And those servers are overseas and have what's called S3 bucket cloud data storage vulnerabilities. And people can enter and change the votes there on the cloud server, and then they can upload them to the specific county level here in this country, because the Scytl company has all the credentials for every server in the counties here. And so they can enter each server of the counties and change the votes from abroad.

It is by the way what everyone has been talking about all this time, and what they have tried to censor saying that the machines were not even connected to the internet.

Then the Department of Homeland Security came along, and the people of Austin realized that what we were telling them was correct. They were horrified and began to try to have a series of classified briefings within their own group in order to get these reports to higher management levels. So these reports went up one or two levels within the administration, and then a solid wall of resistance was formed with the message that we should put this matter aside.

It was in September 2020 when the investigation process within the administration on our reports stopped, so we already knew that the November 3rd elections were going to be stolen. We had already seen it before in the primary elections of 2018 and therefore we knew that anything was possible. Now we simply did not know how many foreign servers would be involved in the switching of votes and in the voting process. We had not seen many foreign servers enter the system and change votes in the past elections, but in this election, of course, we saw thousands of people from all over the world. In fact we have seen data that reflects the intrusion of multitudes of foreign servers into the servers of the US counties.

So we thought that this was going to happen on three levels, we thought there would be massive local fraud, fraud through the voting companies themselves, and by votes injected from abroad. And that's exactly what we saw happen. We collected huge amounts of evidence about what happened, but no court case was ever allowed, this evidence was never allowed to be presented, which is what led to the media myth that there was no evidence of voter fraud, because the judges didn't want to even look at the evidence.

The case of Antrim County in Michigan

In this small county called Antrim in the state of Michigan there are about fifteen thousand people and about seven thousand voted, but the votes were obviously switched from the Republican to the Democratic party, since in this county there have always been approximately 65% of votes to the Republicans and 35% of votes to the Democrats, and the electoral result was completely reversed with 65% of votes to the Democratic Party and 35% to the Republican Party. So, everyone in the city knew that it was a deviation that did not make sense, and therefore this case is still open in court.

Russell Ramsland continues explaining:

"Yes, we were tasked with investigating the case of the Antrim county in Michigan. In fact, I signed the forensic audit report with the collaboration of our team, and that happened because there was a racial motive in the case, and the judge allowed a limited discovery. What came out of it was gruesome enough to allow for further discovery. And then, of course, that report went national because what we found was so horrible. "

In fact, we have been able to do these forensic investigations in other counties on a limited basis, although we have not released that information yet, and there are reasons why we are releasing that information right now and not before.

In fact we have done research in two other counties as well, and the vote switch is like in Antrim, but worse in many ways. So when people vote and scan their ballot, it either goes to the normal ballot box and is voted on, or it goes to what is called an adjudication box. So if It goes to the adjudication box, then whoever is running and controlling the voting system can vote that vote however they want. At Antrim for example, we find vote rejection rates of 82%. Thus, 82% of the votes went to the adjudication box, when the average percentage of votes to adjudicate is normally less than 1%. While in Fulton County, they have admitted that there was an adjudication rate of 93.6%. In these cases it means that the entire election will be decided by the people who ran the system and not by the voters.

In fact, all the voting machines in these elections were connected to the internet and not only those of Dominion.

In fact for these people who say that the vote counting machines are not connected to the internet, we have affidavits from an election judge who showed up at her precinct, and found out that they had uploaded the wrong election data onto her computer, so they called the voting company and they put her on hold. Then the IT support team from another state called her, and within ten minutes they somehow reloaded the correct election data. How can you do that if you are not connected to the Internet?

The fact that these vote counting machines be connected to the internet may be illegal in some cases. I mean, the problem is that in theory the voting system can be trusted because it is not online, but they are clearly online. So we ran a little operation in Dallas during this last election. What we did is that every day we just took the information from the voter records of the people who voted that day in Dallas, as Dallas posted them online. So we had a very large registry of voters in which we did not see how they voted, but we could see everything else: name, where the person lives, when they asked for a vote to be taken at their residence, when they voted, etc. And as you know, these registries are made up of zeros and ones,

There is also a company from Barcelona, Spain, called Scytl, which owns the company called Clarity Election Night Reporting, to which electoral systems companies like Hart, Dominion and others report errors, and then from "Clarity Election Night Reporting" supposedly they only pass on the votes to the media. But using standard white hat tools, we can look and see what is on its server in Frankfurt, Germany, where a malware called "Queues Snatch" is found in an area of its computer.

This malware observes all the information that enters this server and takes the login credentials of each county from the country that is reporting to it, so that once that the server has all those credentials, they can track that county and can access the database of the county from abroad or anywhere they want, and inject changes to the votes as desired.

Dr. Shiva is an Indian-American engineer, politician and entrepreneur (Indian: from India in this case), who has four degrees from the Massachusetts Institute of Technology (MIT), including a Ph.D. in biological engineering, and has received a scholarship Fulbright. In 2018 he ran as an independent candidate for the state of Massachusetts to the US Senate in the primary elections of September the 1st 2018, and explains in the interview with Mike Lindell and specifically in the documentary "Absolute evidence", that it was rare that a person with his engineering and scientific profile and who has four university degrees stood as a candidate for the Senate. He explains how he grew up in India, in a third world country, where he thinks that electoral fraud could occur, but that he did not think at all that it could occur in the United States. Thus for the primary elections to the United States Senate on September the 1st 2018, where according to all the polls he was considered to be the winner, he ended up winning in Fraklin County where the votes in person and with paper ballots are between 80% and the 90% of the total vote, achieving a victory with the 10% of votes more than the other candidate, while in the rest of Massachusetts counties he lost in all of them with 40% of the vote compared to 60% of his opponent. Then he realized that having lost in all counties by exactly the same percentage of votes to his Hispanic opponent, who had won both in counties with a majority of white population and with a majority of black population, was scientifically impossible and It was not a standard deviation of the vote but an anomaly.

He also said on the interview that he is also an expert on this subject since he builds large-scale computer systems, and some of his systems have even been used by the US Senate and by the 1,000 largest companies according to the list of the Fortune magazine. So he is fully aware of the power of electronic systems, and that when a physical process is converted to electronic format, the person who designs this system has immense power.

Then all these reasonings made him begin his investigative trip, after realizing that electoral fraud could take place in the United States. So he started reading as much as he could until September the 9th 2020, eight days after the Senate primary election, and discovered that there are two ways to vote on these electronic voting machines. One in which the person votes, inserts the ballot in the ballot box and **human beings count the paper ballot. That is what happened in Franklin County. But in the other counties they used vote counting tabulating machines, and when the ballot is fed into** the tabulator machine, the paper ballot is turned into an image, called a ballot image, which is no different than when someone takes a photo with an iPhone for example. Then the machine puts the ballot aside, and tries to find out where the circles are on that ballot, that is, the machine counts the images on the ballot and this is how it counts the votes. In this way he realized that for the vote counting tabulating machines the images are the ballots.

Then he discovered that images of a ballot were being created. And then he also found out that in 1974 they passed a law for the federal elections that says that those ballot images should be kept. This was one piece of the puzzle, while the other piece of the puzzle that he discovered was that voting machines as early as 2002 have a feature called the "weighted race feature", which It is integrated into the system and with which the votes of the candidates can be multiplied by a percentage. Then it is possible to multiply the votes obtained by any candidate for example by 2, by 0.5, etc. He also added that regarding this weighted career function and its possibility of multiplying the votes, It can be found in the Diebold voting manual, going to page number two, writing 1.26 in the manual for the 2002 version.

In addition, Dr. Shiva says that they tested and showed that the state of Massachusetts had deleted those images, and that he had to use his over 40 years of experience in computer systems to analyze the data, and thus he realized of a particular anomaly in the Suffolk County, where the majority of people vote for the Democratic Party, and in whose county there was a pattern in the percentage of votes that was constantly repeating, which would only happen statistically one in a 100,000 times.

Then he denounced the state of Massachusetts for this anomaly in the vote count, and the judge accepted the case, which is still open. He also wrote about it on Twitter, a social media platform that did nothing with his publication, but nevertheless the secretary of state together with the National Association of State Electoral Directors contacted Twitter to close his account on the social media platform, and Twitter did so following government orders, in the same way that it happens in countries like China where companies follow government orders.

In addition, Dr. Shiva explains that his case is still open in court, even though they filed a motion of about 200 pages against his case so that the judge would reject it, but the judge gave a restraining order and rejected this motion.

No one has been able to refute his mathematical explanation that the candidates' votes were multiplied by less than 1 in the case of Dr. Shiva, and by a figure greater than 1 in the case of his Hispanic rival in the primary elections for the Massachusetts Senate.

The testimony of the IT scientist Melissa Carone working for Dominion

Melissa Carone is a freelance computer scientist who worked on the electoral recount for the State of Michingan, who said in Mike Lindell's document "Absolute Proof" that Dominion contacted her through her LinkedIn profile to work for IT support on the days of the election, that is on November the 3rd and on November the 4t^{h}.

He tells in this documentary that he worked a total of 26 hours pacing up and down next to Dominion's vote-counting tabulating machines, and that during those 26 hours all the votes that she saw were for Biden and none for Donald Trump. She also explained that Dominion's vote tabulating machines resemble printers in which ballots are fed from the top. These votes were entered in batches of 50 votes, and every once in a while a ballot would get stuck. Everyone who worked for Dominion was in front of computers and would see exactly which ballot had been stuck, but instead of solving the incident correctly, what they did was taking that ballot and putting it back on top of the entire batch of ballots,

Melissa says that at night she realized that a tabulator machine pointed out having more than 400 votes, which should not happen since the machine could not count over 50 votes at a time, which she reported to her superior in Dominion, who happened to be one of the Dominion owners, saying to him that they had a big problem as the machines seemed to count the votes over and over again, to which his superior just told her that he did not want to hear that they had a problem.

<u>Accurate evidence of foreign cyberattacks</u>

Mary Fanning, who is a journalist, writer and researcher on National Intelligence, also intervened in the documentary "Absolute Evidence". Mary Fanny reports that a cybersecurity expert began collecting data as of November the 1st 2020, which is why they collected evidence of foreign cyber attacks before, during and after the elections. In fact, they collected terabytes of information documenting voter fraud, information that was collected from 2,995 US counties in real time.

So in these computer records we can see the day, hour and minute the hacker entered the network, from what IP address exactly, from what computer exactly (source ID), the target IP address, the US state and county targets, the source ID or specific computer that was attacked, the way in which they entered the system, either through credentials or the firewall or both, if the cyberattack was successful or not and the number of votes stolen from Donald Trump.

Most of the IP addresses are from China, in fact more than 66%, while the rest are from servers in Frankfurt, Iran, Serbia, Canada, etc. coinciding with the sworn statements of people from the Italian government's military intelligence, and with the statements of the American Colonel Phil Waldron and Russell Ramsland.

So, for example, in this document that consists of thousands of pages, we can see that on November the 5th 2020 at 07:43:38 in the morning, from the IP address 220.181.132.198 from the CN Chinanet network of the province of Beijing, from the computer with source ID 86054cc63d24, attacked Emmet County in the state of Michigan, specifically at the IP address 66.129.42.43 and computer with ID 04cf6f5c8baa, successfully removing 3,477 votes from Donald Trump.

the magazine itself calls a "shadow conspiracy." That conspiracy involved an alliance of the big capital with the union forces of left-wing groups like Planned Parenthood, with racial lobbies and the mass media with social media platforms.

It was precisely in this last area where it was decided to censor and suppress the content that was not in line with the speech inspired by the conspiracy. It was also decided to use the media as a form of pressure on politicians or of propaganda on public opinion. In those days slogans such as appointing Joe Biden president-elect when he was not legally one were spread.

For example like insisting that he had been declared president-elect by the national press association as if this entity had the least legal jurisdiction in this regard, or spreading the slogan that Donald Trump and the Republicans had not won a single legal battle.

The reality was very different from that reported by the media and the social media platforms. To tell the truth, there were institutions such as the Supreme Court that preferred to disassociate themselves from the matter and not enter into considering the evidence presented, alleging reasons that are not infrequently debatable from a legal perspective. However, where the courts have considered the evidence presented to date, they have agreed with Trump or the Republicans in two out of every 3 cases and as of middle of February 2021, there are still 25 more cases to be resolved.

It is very possible that we will never know that had they taken the trouble to examine the evidence, the elections could have been invalidated in enough places to guarantee the re-election of Donald Trump. It is also very possible that we will never know how the Supreme Court despite the lawsuit filed by the general attorneys of more than twenty states decided not to get to the bottom of the matter, and thus avoid examining the evidence presented.

But we do know to this day that there were instances of the media and social media platforms that launched what seems like a great lie easy to deny, which was that no court had ever agreed with Trump or the Republicans, and that this great lie was repeated by unprofessional foreign correspondents, by lazy journalists, and by interested powers not only in the United States but in the rest of the world.

To this day, most of the population continues to believe that this lie spread everywhere, however the truth is that the administration of justice has proved Donald Trump and the Republicans right in two thirds of the cases where the evidence was examined.

It is truly terrifying to think that Adolf Hitler could have been right in stating that the majority of the people can easily be led to believe in the biggest lies as long as they are not small, but substantially large, as he says in his own book "Mein Kampf" (My fight).

10

Conclusion

The fact that electoral fraud of this magnitude may have occurred in the still leading world power, which is the United States, leads us to wonder if there is still real democracy in any sovereign nation on the planet.

If fair and transparent elections cannot be guaranteed in the United States, nor the freedom of expression of dissenting opinions to the State, starting with the censorship of the former president of the USA Donald Trump himself on Twitter, Facebook and YouTube, we may ask ourselves if real democracy and freedom of expression still exist in any country.

To this day, in a counterintuitive way, it seems that the only thing that can guarantee fair elections without fraud would be voting in person and with paper ballots. While technology should be used for the good of humanity and to guarantee real democracy and freedom of expression in nations, it seems that in the elections the opposite is true, since the technology of vote counting machines and the ease of computer data transmission and recording are simply used to steal the vote of others.

Nor should anyone be proud that with the excuse of "strengthening democracy", the mass media or social media platforms are pressured to censor the opinion of any president or of any opinion that questions the electoral results, since it is precisely when this questioning of the electoral results occurs that the exercise of freedom of expression and democracy are strengthened and not the other way around.

Finally, the battle in these presidential elections of November the 3rd 2020, has been again between patriots and globalists, as Donald Trump himself has already pointed out in his speeches, which I have already explained using some other words in my recently published book on Amazon titled "The Globalist Agenda is real, man-made and dangerous. The great friendship between the Great Reset and the Covid-19 ". So Joe Biden together with the coalition of businessmen and the federations of unions along with left movements would be on the side of the globalists, who ultimately want to impose a new world order through supranational entities, transforming sovereign nations, starting with the United States, in mere protectorates without any authority; Whilst Donald Trump and the majority of Republicans would side with the Patriots, defending the traditional values such as the family, the national culture and the rights of the United States, without submitting themselves to external globalist entities and agendas.

Bibliography and other sources consulted

- Article in the American magazine "Time" published on the internet on February the 4th 2021 and in the magazine itself on February the 15th 2021, entitled "The secret history of the shadow campaign that saved the 2020 election, which can be found at the following link: https://time.com/5936036/secret-2020-election-campaign/

- Program "The Great Reset" on César Vidal TV, entitled "Electoral fraud in the United States and Great Reset. The definitive investigation " (the original title in Spanish is: "Fraude electoral en Estados Unidos y Great Reset. La investigación definitiva").

- Documentary "Absolute Proof" by Mike Lindell about electoral fraud broadcasted on February the 5th 2021 on One America News Network, OANN.

- Telegram channel called "Rafapal" by Spanish journalist Rafael Palacios about news of electoral fraud in the United States.

- Articles from the Spanish newspaper "Libertad digital" on electoral fraud:
https://www.libertaddigital.com/international/united-states/2020-11-20/euu-elections-giuliani-legal-trucks-confidents-smarmatic-corrupted-democratic-officials-6682606/

https://www.libertaddigital.com/internacional/estados-unidos/2020-11-20/la-empresa-barcelonesa-scytl-financiada-por-el-ministerio-de-industria-acusada-de-amanar-las-american-elections-6682478 /

- Document from Riccardo Corsetto, director of the Italian newspaper "L'Unico" on Giuseppe Conte, Leonardo SpA and the United States embassy in Rome being behind the vote switch fraud to remove Donald Trump.

- Regarding Chapter 9 entitled "Results of the legal actions of Donald Trump's team and other US citizens", the study of the lawyer and physicist John Droz Junior can be found at the following link: http://wiseenergy.org/Energy/Election/2020_Election_Cases.htm